50 Camping Recipes for Home

By: Kelly Johnson

Table of Contents

- Campfire Chili
- Foil Packet Lemon Garlic Shrimp
- Grilled Veggie Skewers
- Campfire Quesadillas
- Dutch Oven Lasagna
- Sausage and Potato Foil Packets
- Campfire Pizza
- Foiled-Wrapped Sweet Potatoes
- Hobo Stew
- Campfire Breakfast Burritos
- Grilled Corn on the Cob
- One-Pot Campfire Jambalaya
- Foil Packet Fajitas
- Campfire Mac and Cheese
- Grilled Trout with Lemon and Herbs
- Campfire Tacos
- Dutch Oven Cornbread
- Stuffed Bell Peppers
- Campfire Omelettes
- Grilled Chicken Kabobs
- Garlic Butter Grilled Shrimp
- Dutch Oven Pot Roast
- Campfire Baked Beans
- Caprese Salad Skewers
- Foil Packet Chicken Fajita Bowls
- Cinnamon Sugar Campfire Donuts
- Grilled Portobello Mushrooms
- Campfire Paella
- Sausage and Egg Breakfast Sandwiches
- BBQ Chicken Foil Packets
- Dutch Oven Chicken and Rice
- Grilled Halloumi Skewers
- Campfire Nachos
- Dutch Oven Lemon Blueberry Cake
- Foil Packet Chicken Parmesan

- Campfire Tinfoil Packet Tacos
- Grilled Stuffed Portobello Mushrooms
- Dutch Oven Chicken Pot Pie
- Foil Packet Lemon Garlic Asparagus
- Campfire Banana Boats
- Shrimp and Sausage Foil Packets
- Grilled Caesar Salad
- Dutch Oven Pumpkin Bread
- Foil Packet Teriyaki Salmon
- Campfire TInfoil Packet Bruschetta Chicken
- Dutch Oven S'mores Cake
- Grilled Zucchini Ribbon Salad
- Campfire Biscuits and Gravy
- Dutch Oven Peach Cobbler
- Foil Packet Teriyaki Veggie Bowls

Campfire Chili

Ingredients:

- 1 lb ground beef
- 1 onion, diced
- 3 cloves garlic, minced
- 1 bell pepper, diced
- 1 can (14 oz) diced tomatoes
- 1 can (14 oz) kidney beans, drained and rinsed
- 1 can (14 oz) black beans, drained and rinsed
- 1 can (14 oz) tomato sauce
- 2 tablespoons tomato paste
- 2 teaspoons chili powder
- 1 teaspoon cumin
- 1 teaspoon paprika
- 1/2 teaspoon oregano
- Salt and pepper to taste
- Optional toppings: shredded cheese, sour cream, green onions, chopped cilantro

Instructions:

Prepare the Campfire:
- Set up your campfire and let it burn down to hot coals. Alternatively, you can use a portable camp stove.

Cook the Ground Beef:
- In a large cast-iron skillet or Dutch oven, cook the ground beef over the campfire or camp stove until browned. Drain excess fat if necessary.

Add Aromatics:
- Add diced onions and minced garlic to the skillet. Cook until the onions are translucent.

Add Vegetables:
- Stir in diced bell pepper and cook until softened.

Combine Ingredients:
- Add diced tomatoes, kidney beans, black beans, tomato sauce, and tomato paste to the skillet. Stir well to combine.

Season the Chili:

- Sprinkle chili powder, cumin, paprika, oregano, salt, and pepper over the mixture. Stir to evenly distribute the spices.

Simmer:
- Allow the chili to simmer over the campfire or camp stove for at least 30 minutes, stirring occasionally.

Check Consistency:
- If the chili becomes too thick, you can add a little water to achieve your desired consistency.

Serve:
- Once the flavors have melded and the chili is heated through, ladle it into bowls.

Top and Enjoy:
- Garnish with your favorite toppings like shredded cheese, sour cream, green onions, or chopped cilantro. Serve hot and enjoy your delicious campfire chili!

Note: Feel free to customize this recipe by adding more spices, adjusting the heat level, or including other favorite chili ingredients. Enjoy this hearty and warming meal on your outdoor adventure!

Foil Packet Lemon Garlic Shrimp

Ingredients:

- 1 lb large shrimp, peeled and deveined
- 2 tablespoons olive oil
- 4 cloves garlic, minced
- 1 teaspoon lemon zest
- 2 tablespoons fresh lemon juice
- 1 teaspoon dried oregano
- Salt and pepper to taste
- 1/2 teaspoon red pepper flakes (optional for a bit of heat)
- 2 tablespoons fresh parsley, chopped
- Lemon slices for garnish
- Foil sheets for packets

Instructions:

Preheat the Grill:
- Preheat your grill to medium-high heat. If you're cooking over an open flame, ensure you have hot coals.

Prepare Foil Packets:
- Tear off large sheets of foil (about 12 inches in length) and fold them in half to create a double layer. This will help prevent the packets from tearing during cooking.

Marinate the Shrimp:
- In a bowl, combine shrimp, olive oil, minced garlic, lemon zest, lemon juice, oregano, salt, pepper, and red pepper flakes (if using). Toss the shrimp until evenly coated with the marinade.

Assemble Foil Packets:
- Divide the marinated shrimp evenly among the foil sheets, placing them in the center.

Fold and Seal Packets:
- Fold the foil over the shrimp, creating a packet. Seal the edges tightly to ensure the juices stay inside during cooking.

Grill the Packets:
- Place the foil packets on the preheated grill or over the campfire. Cook for about 8-10 minutes, or until the shrimp are opaque and cooked through.

Check for Doneness:

- Carefully open one of the packets to check the doneness of the shrimp. They should be pink and opaque.

Garnish and Serve:
- Carefully open the foil packets, being cautious of the hot steam. Sprinkle chopped fresh parsley over the shrimp and garnish with lemon slices.

Serve Warm:
- Serve the lemon garlic shrimp directly from the foil packets. You can pair them with rice, pasta, or crusty bread to soak up the delicious juices.

Enjoy Outdoors:
- Whether you're camping or having a backyard barbecue, these foil packet lemon garlic shrimp make for a flavorful and hassle-free outdoor meal.

Grilled Veggie Skewers

Ingredients:

- Assorted vegetables, cut into bite-sized pieces (e.g., bell peppers, zucchini, cherry tomatoes, red onions, mushrooms)
- 2 tablespoons olive oil
- 2 cloves garlic, minced
- 1 teaspoon dried Italian herbs (rosemary, thyme, oregano)
- Salt and pepper to taste
- Wooden skewers, soaked in water for at least 30 minutes

Instructions:

Preheat the Grill:
- Preheat your grill to medium-high heat.

Prepare the Vegetables:
- Wash and cut the vegetables into uniform, bite-sized pieces. This ensures even cooking.

Make the Marinade:
- In a bowl, whisk together olive oil, minced garlic, dried Italian herbs, salt, and pepper. This will be the marinade for your veggies.

Marinate the Vegetables:
- Place the cut vegetables in a large bowl and toss them with the marinade, ensuring all pieces are well-coated. Allow the vegetables to marinate for at least 15-20 minutes.

Assemble the Skewers:
- Thread the marinated vegetables onto the soaked wooden skewers, alternating the varieties for colorful and flavorful skewers.

Brush with Remaining Marinade:
- Before grilling, brush the skewers with any remaining marinade to enhance the flavor.

Grill the Skewers:
- Place the skewers on the preheated grill. Grill for about 10-15 minutes, turning occasionally, or until the vegetables are tender and slightly charred.

Check for Doneness:
- Test the doneness of the vegetables by inserting a fork or knife into them. They should be tender but not mushy.

Serve Warm:
- Remove the skewers from the grill and let them rest for a minute. Serve the grilled veggie skewers warm.

Optional Garnish:
- Garnish the skewers with additional herbs or a drizzle of balsamic glaze for extra flavor.

Enjoy:
- Whether served as a side dish, appetizer, or a main course, these grilled veggie skewers are a delicious and healthy addition to your outdoor dining experience.

Campfire Quesadillas

Ingredients:

- Flour tortillas
- Cooked and shredded chicken (pre-cooked at home or canned chicken for convenience)
- Shredded cheese (cheddar, Monterey Jack, or a blend)
- Diced tomatoes
- Diced bell peppers (assorted colors)
- Diced red onion
- Sliced jalapeños (optional for heat)
- Olive oil or cooking spray
- Salsa, guacamole, or sour cream for serving (optional)

Instructions:

Prep Ingredients:
- Pre-chop all the vegetables and have them ready for assembly.

Assemble Quesadillas:
- Place a tortilla on a flat surface. On one half of the tortilla, layer shredded chicken, shredded cheese, diced tomatoes, bell peppers, red onion, and jalapeños if desired.

Fold and Seal:
- Fold the other half of the tortilla over the filling to create a half-moon shape. Press the edges together to seal.

Create Individual Packets:
- Wrap each filled tortilla in aluminum foil to create individual packets. This will make it easier to handle on the campfire.

Preheat the Grill or Campfire:
- Preheat your grill or set up a campfire with hot coals.

Cook the Quesadillas:
- Place the foil-wrapped quesadillas on the grill grates or directly onto the hot coals. Cook for about 5-7 minutes on each side, or until the tortillas are crispy and the cheese is melted.

Check for Doneness:
- Carefully open one foil packet to check the doneness of the quesadilla. Ensure that the cheese is fully melted and the ingredients are heated through.

Serve and Enjoy:
- Remove the quesadillas from the foil packets, cut into wedges, and serve with your favorite condiments such as salsa, guacamole, or sour cream.

Optional Variation:
- Experiment with different fillings like black beans, corn, or different types of cheese to suit your preferences.

Enjoy the Outdoors:
- Whether you're camping or having a backyard cookout, these campfire quesadillas are a quick, customizable, and delicious meal to enjoy outdoors.

Dutch Oven Lasagna

Ingredients:

- 1 lb ground beef or Italian sausage
- 1 onion, finely chopped
- 3 cloves garlic, minced
- 1 can (28 oz) crushed tomatoes
- 1 can (14 oz) tomato sauce
- 1 can (6 oz) tomato paste
- 2 teaspoons dried oregano
- 2 teaspoons dried basil
- Salt and pepper to taste
- 9 lasagna noodles, uncooked
- 1 1/2 cups ricotta cheese
- 2 cups shredded mozzarella cheese
- 1 cup grated Parmesan cheese
- Fresh basil or parsley for garnish (optional)

Instructions:

Prepare the Dutch Oven:
- Preheat your Dutch oven over medium heat by placing hot coals on the bottom and adding a few to the lid for top heat.

Brown the Meat:
- In the Dutch oven, brown the ground beef or Italian sausage, breaking it up into small pieces. Add chopped onions and minced garlic, and cook until the onions are translucent.

Add Tomato Sauce:
- Pour in crushed tomatoes, tomato sauce, and tomato paste. Stir well to combine.

Season the Sauce:
- Add dried oregano, dried basil, salt, and pepper to the sauce. Stir and let it simmer for about 10-15 minutes to allow the flavors to meld.

Layer the Lasagna:
- Break the lasagna noodles into smaller pieces and layer them on top of the sauce. Make sure the noodles are evenly distributed.

Add Ricotta and Cheese:

- Dollop ricotta cheese over the noodles and sprinkle with mozzarella and Parmesan cheeses.

Repeat Layers:
- Repeat the layers until you run out of ingredients, finishing with a layer of cheese on top.

Cover and Cook:
- Place the lid on the Dutch oven and let the lasagna cook over the hot coals for about 30-40 minutes. Rotate the Dutch oven occasionally for even cooking.

Check for Doneness:
- Check the lasagna by inserting a knife into the center. If the noodles are tender and the cheese is melted and bubbly, it's ready.

Garnish and Serve:
- Garnish with fresh basil or parsley if desired. Serve the Dutch Oven Lasagna directly from the pot.

Enjoy Outdoors:
- Whether you're camping or enjoying a backyard gathering, this Dutch Oven Lasagna brings the comfort of a classic Italian dish to the great outdoors.

Sausage and Potato Foil Packets

Ingredients:

- 1 lb smoked sausage or kielbasa, sliced
- 4 cups baby potatoes, halved or quartered
- 1 onion, thinly sliced
- 1 bell pepper, thinly sliced (optional)
- 2 cloves garlic, minced
- 2 tablespoons olive oil
- 1 teaspoon dried thyme
- 1 teaspoon dried rosemary
- Salt and pepper to taste
- Fresh parsley for garnish (optional)

Instructions:

Preheat the Grill or Oven:
- Preheat your grill to medium-high heat or your oven to 400°F (200°C).

Prepare Foil Packets:
- Tear off large sheets of aluminum foil (about 12 inches in length). You'll need one sheet for each packet.

Combine Ingredients:
- In a large bowl, combine sliced sausage, halved baby potatoes, sliced onion, sliced bell pepper (if using), and minced garlic.

Drizzle with Olive Oil:
- Drizzle olive oil over the sausage and potato mixture. Toss the ingredients to ensure even coating.

Season the Mixture:
- Sprinkle dried thyme, dried rosemary, salt, and pepper over the mixture. Toss again to evenly distribute the seasonings.

Assemble Foil Packets:
- Divide the sausage and potato mixture among the foil sheets, placing it in the center of each sheet.

Seal the Packets:
- Fold the foil over the ingredients to create packets. Seal the edges tightly to prevent steam from escaping during cooking.

Grill or Bake:

- Place the foil packets on the preheated grill grates or in the oven. Grill for about 20-25 minutes or bake for 30-35 minutes, or until the potatoes are tender.

Check for Doneness:
- Carefully open one packet to check the doneness of the potatoes. They should be easily pierced with a fork.

Garnish and Serve:
- Open the foil packets, and if desired, garnish the sausage and potato mixture with fresh parsley. Serve directly from the packets.

Enjoy:
- Whether you're camping, grilling in the backyard, or using the oven, these Sausage and Potato Foil Packets make for a delicious and hassle-free meal with minimal cleanup.

Campfire Pizza

Ingredients:

For the Dough:

- 2 cups all-purpose flour
- 1/2 teaspoon salt
- 1 cup unsalted butter, cold and cut into small cubes
- 1/2 cup cold water

For the Filling:

- 2 cups cooked turkey, shredded or diced
- 1/2 cup cranberry sauce
- 1/4 cup cream cheese, softened
- 1/4 cup green onions, chopped
- Salt and black pepper, to taste

For Assembly:

- 1 egg, beaten (for egg wash)
- Sesame seeds (optional, for garnish)

Instructions:

For the Dough:

In a large bowl, whisk together the flour and salt.
Add the cold, cubed butter to the flour mixture. Use your fingers or a pastry cutter to incorporate the butter until the mixture resembles coarse crumbs.
Gradually add the cold water, mixing until the dough comes together. Form the dough into a ball, wrap it in plastic wrap, and refrigerate for at least 30 minutes.

For the Filling:

In a mixing bowl, combine the cooked turkey, cranberry sauce, cream cheese, and chopped green onions. Season with salt and black pepper to taste. Mix until well combined.

Assembly:

    Preheat the oven to 375°F (190°C).
    On a floured surface, roll out the chilled dough to about 1/8 inch thickness.
    Use a round cutter or a glass to cut out circles from the dough.
    Place a spoonful of the turkey and cranberry filling in the center of each dough circle.
    Fold the dough over the filling, creating a half-moon shape. Seal the edges by pressing them together with a fork.
    Place the hand pies on a baking sheet lined with parchment paper.
    Brush the tops of the hand pies with beaten egg and sprinkle with sesame seeds if desired.
    Bake in the preheated oven for 15-20 minutes or until the hand pies are golden brown.
    Allow the Turkey and Cranberry Hand Pies to cool slightly before serving.
    Enjoy these handheld delights as a festive and flavorful appetizer or snack!

These Turkey and Cranberry Hand Pies are a delightful and convenient way to enjoy the flavors of a holiday meal in a handheld form. The combination of tender turkey, sweet cranberry sauce, and creamy cream cheese encased in a flaky pastry creates a perfect bite-sized treat. Serve them as a festive appetizer or enjoy them as a portable snack during the holiday season. The sesame seed garnish adds a subtle crunch to each hand pie.

Foiled-Wrapped Sweet Potatoes

Ingredients:

- 4 medium-sized sweet potatoes
- 2 tablespoons olive oil
- Salt and pepper, to taste
- Optional toppings: butter, brown sugar, cinnamon, marshmallows, chopped nuts, or herbs

Instructions:

Preheat your oven to 400°F (200°C).
Wash and scrub the sweet potatoes thoroughly to remove any dirt.
Pierce each sweet potato several times with a fork to allow steam to escape during baking.
Place each sweet potato on a piece of aluminum foil large enough to wrap it completely.
Drizzle each sweet potato with olive oil and sprinkle with salt and pepper. You can also rub the oil, salt, and pepper onto the sweet potatoes to coat them evenly.
Wrap each sweet potato tightly in the foil, ensuring that the edges are sealed.
Place the foil-wrapped sweet potatoes directly on the oven rack or on a baking sheet.
Bake in the preheated oven for 45-60 minutes, or until the sweet potatoes are tender. The baking time may vary depending on the size of the sweet potatoes.
Carefully unwrap the foil, and test the sweet potatoes for doneness by inserting a fork or knife into the center; it should slide in easily.
Once cooked, serve the foiled-wrapped sweet potatoes hot.
Optionally, add your favorite toppings such as butter, brown sugar, cinnamon, marshmallows, chopped nuts, or herbs.
Enjoy these perfectly baked and customizable sweet potatoes!

These Foiled-Wrapped Sweet Potatoes are a simple and delicious way to prepare this nutritious and versatile root vegetable. The foil wrapping helps the sweet potatoes cook evenly and retain their natural sweetness. You can customize them with various toppings to suit your taste, making them a delightful side dish for any meal. Whether served with a savory dinner or as a sweet treat, these foil-wrapped sweet potatoes are sure to be a hit.

Hobo Stew

Ingredients:

- 1 pound ground beef or ground turkey
- 1 onion, diced
- 2 cloves garlic, minced
- 4 cups mixed vegetables (carrots, potatoes, bell peppers, corn, green beans, etc.), diced
- 1 can (15 ounces) diced tomatoes, undrained
- 1 can (15 ounces) tomato sauce
- 2 cups beef or vegetable broth
- 1 teaspoon dried thyme
- 1 teaspoon dried rosemary
- Salt and pepper, to taste
- Optional: Worcestershire sauce or hot sauce for added flavor

Instructions:

In a large skillet or Dutch oven, cook the ground beef or turkey over medium heat until browned. Drain any excess fat.
Add diced onions and minced garlic to the skillet, and sauté until the onions are translucent.
Stir in the mixed vegetables, diced tomatoes (with their juice), tomato sauce, and beef or vegetable broth.
Season the stew with dried thyme, dried rosemary, salt, and pepper. Add Worcestershire sauce or hot sauce if desired for extra flavor.
Bring the stew to a boil, then reduce the heat to low. Cover and simmer for 20-30 minutes, or until the vegetables are tender.
Taste and adjust the seasoning if needed.
Serve the Hobo Stew hot, and enjoy this hearty and flavorful one-pot meal.

Hobo Stew is a comforting and versatile one-pot dish that allows for flexibility in ingredient choices based on what you have available. It's a convenient and hearty meal, perfect for camping or a cozy family dinner. The combination of ground meat, vegetables, and savory seasonings creates a satisfying stew that can be easily customized to suit your taste preferences. Serve it with crusty bread or over rice for a complete and wholesome meal.

Campfire Breakfast Burritos

Ingredients:

- 8 large flour tortillas
- 8 large eggs
- 1 pound breakfast sausage, cooked and crumbled
- 1 cup shredded cheddar cheese
- 1 cup diced tomatoes
- 1 cup diced bell peppers (any color)
- 1/2 cup diced red onion
- 1/2 cup chopped fresh cilantro
- Salt and pepper, to taste
- Salsa, for serving (optional)
- Avocado slices, for serving (optional)

Instructions:

Prepare a campfire or portable grill with medium heat.
In a large skillet or cast-iron pan, scramble the eggs over the campfire or portable grill. Season with salt and pepper to taste.
Lay out each tortilla on a flat surface.
Assemble the burritos by placing a portion of scrambled eggs in the center of each tortilla.
Add a portion of cooked sausage, shredded cheddar cheese, diced tomatoes, diced bell peppers, diced red onion, and chopped cilantro onto the eggs.
Optional: Add salsa or avocado slices for extra flavor.
Fold the sides of the tortilla in and then roll it up tightly to create a burrito.
Wrap each burrito in aluminum foil.
Place the foil-wrapped breakfast burritos on the campfire grate or grill. Cook for about 5-7 minutes, turning occasionally, until the burritos are heated through and the cheese is melted.
Carefully unwrap the foil and check if the burritos are hot and well-cooked.
Serve the Campfire Breakfast Burritos hot and enjoy this delicious and portable breakfast!

These Campfire Breakfast Burritos are a convenient and tasty way to start your day during camping trips or outdoor adventures. The combination of scrambled eggs, savory sausage, cheese, and fresh vegetables wrapped in a warm tortilla makes for a satisfying and hearty breakfast. You can customize the fillings based on your preferences, and the burritos can be easily wrapped in foil for mess-free enjoyment. Whether by the campfire or at home, these breakfast burritos are sure to be a crowd-pleaser.

Grilled Corn on the Cob

Ingredients:

- Fresh corn on the cob, husks intact
- Butter, softened
- Salt and pepper, to taste
- Optional: Fresh herbs (such as parsley or cilantro), grated Parmesan cheese, chili powder, or lime wedges for seasoning

Instructions:

Preheat your grill to medium-high heat.
Peel back the husks of the corn without removing them entirely. Remove the silk threads from the corn.
Spread a thin layer of softened butter over each corn cob. Season with salt and pepper to taste.
Optionally, sprinkle fresh herbs, grated Parmesan cheese, chili powder, or a squeeze of lime juice over the buttered corn for added flavor.
Pull the husks back up over the corn to cover it.
Place the prepared corn on the grill, placing the covered side down.
Grill the corn for about 15-20 minutes, turning occasionally, until the corn is tender and has a slightly charred appearance.
Carefully remove the corn from the grill.
Peel back the husks and serve the Grilled Corn on the Cob hot.
Optionally, add more butter or seasoning before serving.

Grilled Corn on the Cob is a classic and delicious side dish that highlights the natural sweetness of fresh corn with a smoky flavor from the grill. The butter and seasonings add extra richness and enhance the overall taste. This simple and versatile recipe is perfect for summer cookouts or anytime you want to enjoy the flavor of grilled corn. Serve it alongside your favorite grilled meats or as a standalone snack for a delightful outdoor dining experience.

One-Pot Campfire Jambalaya

Ingredients:

- 1 pound andouille sausage, sliced
- 1 pound chicken thighs, boneless and skinless, cut into bite-sized pieces
- 1 large onion, diced
- 1 bell pepper, diced
- 3 celery ribs, chopped
- 3 cloves garlic, minced
- 1 can (14 ounces) diced tomatoes, undrained
- 1 cup long-grain white rice
- 2 cups chicken broth
- 1 teaspoon dried thyme
- 1 teaspoon dried oregano
- 1 teaspoon paprika
- 1/2 teaspoon cayenne pepper (adjust to taste)
- Salt and black pepper, to taste
- 1 pound large shrimp, peeled and deveined
- Green onions, chopped (for garnish)
- Fresh parsley, chopped (for garnish)

Instructions:

Heat a large cast-iron Dutch oven over a campfire or portable grill.
Add sliced andouille sausage to the Dutch oven and cook until browned.
Add the chicken pieces to the sausage in the Dutch oven. Cook until the chicken is browned on all sides.
Stir in diced onion, bell pepper, celery, and minced garlic. Sauté until the vegetables are softened.
Add diced tomatoes (with their juice) to the Dutch oven, along with rice, chicken broth, dried thyme, dried oregano, paprika, cayenne pepper, salt, and black pepper. Stir to combine.
Bring the mixture to a boil, then reduce the heat to low. Cover the Dutch oven with a lid and let it simmer for about 20-25 minutes, or until the rice is cooked and has absorbed the liquid.

Add the peeled and deveined shrimp to the top of the jambalaya mixture. Cover and cook for an additional 5-7 minutes, or until the shrimp are pink and cooked through.

Remove the Dutch oven from the heat and let it rest for a few minutes.

Garnish the Campfire Jambalaya with chopped green onions and fresh parsley.

Serve the flavorful and hearty One-Pot Campfire Jambalaya hot and enjoy your outdoor feast!

This One-Pot Campfire Jambalaya is a delicious and satisfying dish perfect for outdoor cooking adventures. Packed with a variety of proteins, aromatic vegetables, and flavorful spices, this jambalaya captures the essence of the classic Louisiana dish. Whether you're camping, tailgating, or just enjoying a backyard cookout, this one-pot recipe simplifies the cooking process while delivering bold and comforting flavors. Garnish with green onions and fresh parsley for a finishing touch.

Foil Packet Fajitas

Ingredients:

- 1 pound chicken breasts, thinly sliced
- 1 red bell pepper, sliced
- 1 green bell pepper, sliced
- 1 onion, sliced
- 2 cloves garlic, minced
- 2 tablespoons fajita seasoning
- 2 tablespoons vegetable oil
- Juice of 1 lime
- Salt and pepper, to taste
- Flour tortillas, for serving
- Optional toppings: shredded cheese, sour cream, guacamole, salsa, cilantro

Instructions:

Preheat your grill or oven to medium-high heat.

In a bowl, combine sliced chicken, red bell pepper, green bell pepper, onion, minced garlic, fajita seasoning, vegetable oil, lime juice, salt, and pepper. Toss everything together until the chicken and vegetables are well-coated.

Tear off sheets of aluminum foil, each large enough to wrap a portion of the fajita mixture.

Divide the fajita mixture among the foil sheets, placing a portion in the center of each.

Fold the sides of the foil over the fajita mixture and seal the edges to create a packet.

Place the foil packets on the grill or in the oven. Cook for about 15-20 minutes, turning once halfway through, or until the chicken is cooked through and the vegetables are tender.

Carefully open the foil packets, being mindful of the hot steam.

Serve the foil packet fajitas in warm flour tortillas.

Optional: Garnish with shredded cheese, sour cream, guacamole, salsa, and cilantro.

Enjoy these delicious and hassle-free Foil Packet Fajitas with your favorite toppings!

Foil Packet Fajitas are a convenient and flavorful way to enjoy this classic Tex-Mex dish. The foil packets simplify the cooking process and allow the chicken and vegetables to cook together, locking in the delicious fajita flavors. Serve the contents in warm flour tortillas and customize with your preferred toppings for a satisfying and mess-free meal. Whether you're grilling outdoors or using the oven, foil packet fajitas are a great option for easy and delicious weeknight dinners or camping meals.

Campfire Mac and Cheese

Ingredients:

- 8 ounces elbow macaroni
- 2 cups shredded sharp cheddar cheese
- 1/2 cup grated Parmesan cheese
- 3 cups milk
- 1/4 cup butter
- 3 tablespoons all-purpose flour
- 1/2 teaspoon salt
- 1/4 teaspoon black pepper
- 1/4 teaspoon paprika
- Optional: Diced cooked bacon, chopped green onions, or breadcrumbs for topping

Instructions:

Cook the elbow macaroni according to the package instructions, but slightly undercook it, as it will continue to cook while being heated over the campfire.
In a large pot or Dutch oven, melt the butter over the campfire or portable grill. Stir in the flour to create a roux, cooking for 1-2 minutes until lightly golden.
Gradually whisk in the milk to avoid lumps. Cook and stir until the mixture thickens.
Add shredded cheddar cheese and grated Parmesan cheese to the milk mixture. Stir until the cheese is melted and the sauce is smooth.
Season the cheese sauce with salt, black pepper, and paprika. Adjust the seasonings to taste.
Fold in the slightly undercooked elbow macaroni, ensuring that the pasta is well-coated with the cheese sauce.
If desired, mix in diced cooked bacon for added flavor.
Optionally, sprinkle chopped green onions or breadcrumbs over the top for a crunchy topping.
Cover the pot or Dutch oven and let the Campfire Mac and Cheese cook for a few more minutes, allowing the flavors to meld.
Serve the cheesy goodness hot and enjoy your campfire comfort food!

Campfire Mac and Cheese is a delicious and comforting dish that brings the classic comfort of macaroni and cheese to your outdoor adventures. The creamy cheese sauce is made over the campfire or portable grill, and the elbow macaroni cooks right in the sauce, creating a convenient one-pot meal. Customize with optional toppings like bacon, green onions, or breadcrumbs for added flavor and texture. Whether you're camping, tailgating, or enjoying a backyard cookout, Campfire Mac and Cheese is a crowd-pleaser for all ages.

Grilled Trout with Lemon and Herbs

Ingredients:

- 4 whole trout, cleaned and gutted
- 2 lemons, thinly sliced
- 1/4 cup fresh parsley, chopped
- 2 tablespoons fresh dill, chopped
- 2 tablespoons olive oil
- Salt and pepper, to taste
- Lemon wedges, for serving

Instructions:

Preheat your grill to medium-high heat.
Rinse the trout under cold water and pat them dry with paper towels.
Season the inside and outside of each trout with salt and pepper.
Stuff the cavity of each trout with lemon slices, fresh parsley, and fresh dill.
Brush the outside of the trout with olive oil, ensuring they are well-coated.
Place the trout on the preheated grill and cook for about 4-5 minutes per side, or until the fish is cooked through and easily flakes with a fork.
While grilling, baste the trout with any remaining olive oil and juices from the lemon and herbs.
Carefully transfer the grilled trout to a serving platter.
Garnish with additional chopped herbs and lemon wedges.
Serve the Grilled Trout with Lemon and Herbs hot and enjoy this simple and flavorful dish!

Grilled Trout with Lemon and Herbs is a light and refreshing dish that showcases the natural flavors of the fish enhanced with the brightness of lemon and the aromatic herbs. The grilling method adds a smoky flavor and crispy skin to the trout, creating a delightful and healthy meal. This recipe is perfect for a summer barbecue or a cozy dinner by the grill. Serve the grilled trout alongside your favorite side dishes for a complete and satisfying dining experience.

Campfire Tacos

Ingredients:

- 1 pound ground beef or ground turkey
- 1 packet taco seasoning
- 1 cup water
- 1 can (15 ounces) black beans, drained and rinsed
- 1 cup corn kernels (fresh or frozen)
- 1 cup diced tomatoes
- 1 cup shredded lettuce
- 1 cup shredded cheddar cheese
- 1/2 cup diced red onions
- 1/4 cup chopped fresh cilantro
- 8 small flour tortillas
- Sour cream, salsa, and lime wedges for serving

Instructions:

Heat a cast-iron skillet or a campfire-friendly pan over the campfire or portable grill.
Cook the ground beef or turkey in the skillet until browned, breaking it apart with a spoon.
Drain any excess fat from the meat, if necessary.
In a small bowl, mix the taco seasoning with water and add it to the cooked meat. Stir well and let it simmer until the sauce thickens.
Add black beans and corn to the skillet, cooking for an additional 2-3 minutes until heated through.
Warm the flour tortillas over the campfire or on the grill for about 30 seconds per side.
Assemble the Campfire Tacos by spooning the meat mixture onto each tortilla.
Top with diced tomatoes, shredded lettuce, cheddar cheese, diced red onions, and chopped cilantro.
Serve the tacos with sour cream, salsa, and lime wedges on the side.
Enjoy these delicious and customizable Campfire Tacos with your favorite toppings!

Campfire Tacos are a fun and easy outdoor meal that brings the flavors of your favorite taco night to the great outdoors. The seasoned meat, black beans, and corn create a hearty and flavorful filling, while the toppings add freshness and crunch. Whether you're camping, hiking, or simply enjoying a backyard bonfire, these tacos are a crowd-pleaser. Customize with your preferred toppings and sauces for a personalized taco experience around the campfire.

Dutch Oven Cornbread

Ingredients:

- 1 cup yellow cornmeal
- 1 cup all-purpose flour
- 1 tablespoon baking powder
- 1/2 teaspoon baking soda
- 1/2 teaspoon salt
- 1 cup buttermilk
- 1/4 cup unsalted butter, melted
- 1/4 cup vegetable oil
- 2 large eggs
- Optional: 1 cup corn kernels (fresh, frozen, or canned)

Instructions:

Preheat your Dutch oven by placing coals on top and beneath it, creating a hot oven environment.
In a large bowl, whisk together the cornmeal, flour, baking powder, baking soda, and salt.
In a separate bowl, whisk together buttermilk, melted butter, vegetable oil, and eggs.
Pour the wet ingredients into the dry ingredients and stir until just combined. If using, fold in the corn kernels.
Grease the bottom and sides of the preheated Dutch oven with butter or oil.
Pour the cornbread batter into the Dutch oven, spreading it evenly.
Place the lid on the Dutch oven and arrange hot coals on top.
Bake the cornbread for approximately 20-25 minutes or until a toothpick inserted into the center comes out clean.
Carefully remove the Dutch oven from the heat.
Allow the cornbread to cool slightly before slicing and serving.
Enjoy your Dutch Oven Cornbread as a side dish to complement your outdoor meals!

Dutch Oven Cornbread is a classic and hearty addition to your outdoor cooking repertoire. The Dutch oven creates a perfect environment for baking, resulting in a golden and slightly crispy exterior while maintaining a moist and flavorful interior. Whether you're camping or enjoying a backyard barbecue, this cornbread pairs well with various dishes, from chili to grilled meats. Customize it by adding corn kernels for an extra burst of sweetness and texture.

Stuffed Bell Peppers

Ingredients:

- 4 large bell peppers, halved and seeds removed
- 1 pound ground beef or turkey
- 1 cup cooked rice (white or brown)
- 1 can (15 ounces) black beans, drained and rinsed
- 1 cup corn kernels (fresh, frozen, or canned)
- 1 cup diced tomatoes
- 1 cup shredded cheddar cheese
- 1/2 cup diced onions
- 2 cloves garlic, minced
- 1 teaspoon chili powder
- 1 teaspoon ground cumin
- 1/2 teaspoon paprika
- Salt and pepper, to taste
- Fresh cilantro or parsley, chopped (for garnish)

Instructions:

Preheat your oven to 375°F (190°C).
In a large skillet, cook the ground beef or turkey over medium heat until browned. Drain any excess fat.
Add diced onions and minced garlic to the skillet, cooking until the onions are softened.
Stir in black beans, corn, diced tomatoes, cooked rice, chili powder, ground cumin, paprika, salt, and pepper. Cook for an additional 5 minutes to let the flavors meld.
Place the halved bell peppers in a baking dish.
Spoon the stuffing mixture into each pepper half, pressing it down gently.
Top each stuffed pepper with shredded cheddar cheese.
Cover the baking dish with aluminum foil.
Bake in the preheated oven for 25-30 minutes or until the peppers are tender.
Remove the foil and bake for an additional 5-10 minutes, allowing the cheese to melt and become bubbly.
Garnish with chopped fresh cilantro or parsley.
Serve the Stuffed Bell Peppers hot and enjoy this flavorful and satisfying dish!

Stuffed Bell Peppers are a delicious and versatile dish that can be easily prepared in the oven, making them a great option for a comforting and wholesome meal. The combination of ground meat, rice, beans, and veggies creates a hearty stuffing, while the bell peppers add a vibrant and nutritious touch. Customize the filling to suit your preferences and enjoy these Stuffed Bell Peppers as a standalone meal or alongside your favorite side dishes.

Campfire Omelettes

Ingredients:

- Eggs (2-3 per omelette)
- Salt and pepper, to taste
- Fillings of your choice:
    - Diced bell peppers
    - Diced onions
    - Sliced mushrooms
    - Shredded cheese (cheddar, mozzarella, or your favorite)
    - Cooked ham, bacon, or sausage
    - Fresh herbs (chives, parsley, or cilantro)

Instructions:

Prepare your campfire or portable grill, ensuring you have a bed of hot coals.
In a bowl, whisk the eggs and season with salt and pepper.
Tear off a sheet of heavy-duty aluminum foil for each omelette.
Place the foil sheets on a flat surface and fold up the edges to create a shallow "boat" shape.
Pour the whisked eggs into each foil boat.
Add your chosen fillings to the eggs. Distribute the ingredients evenly.
Carefully fold the foil over the eggs and fillings, creating a sealed packet.
Place the foil packets on the hot coals, avoiding direct contact with flames.
Cook for 10-15 minutes, periodically checking for doneness. The omelette is ready when the eggs are set and no longer runny.
Carefully open the foil packets, allowing steam to escape.
Slide the Campfire Omelettes onto a plate, and garnish with additional herbs if desired.
Serve the omelettes hot and enjoy your customizable campfire breakfast!

Campfire Omelettes are a convenient and customizable way to enjoy a hearty breakfast outdoors. The foil packet method ensures even cooking and easy cleanup, making it perfect for camping or any outdoor adventure. Customize the omelettes with your favorite fillings, and let each person create their personalized breakfast masterpiece. The smoky flavor from cooking over the campfire adds an extra dimension to this classic breakfast dish.

Grilled Chicken Kabobs

Ingredients:

- 1.5 pounds boneless, skinless chicken breasts, cut into bite-sized cubes
- 1/4 cup olive oil
- 3 tablespoons soy sauce
- 2 tablespoons honey
- 2 cloves garlic, minced
- 1 teaspoon ground cumin
- 1 teaspoon smoked paprika
- 1 teaspoon onion powder
- 1/2 teaspoon cayenne pepper (adjust to taste)
- Salt and pepper, to taste
- Vegetables of your choice, cut into chunks (bell peppers, cherry tomatoes, red onions, zucchini, mushrooms, etc.)
- Wooden or metal skewers

Instructions:

If using wooden skewers, soak them in water for at least 30 minutes to prevent burning during grilling.

In a bowl, whisk together olive oil, soy sauce, honey, minced garlic, ground cumin, smoked paprika, onion powder, cayenne pepper, salt, and pepper to create the marinade.

Place the chicken cubes in a resealable plastic bag or a shallow dish and pour half of the marinade over the chicken. Reserve the remaining marinade for basting.

Marinate the chicken for at least 30 minutes to allow the flavors to infuse.

Preheat your grill to medium-high heat.

Thread the marinated chicken and vegetables onto the skewers, alternating between chicken and vegetables.

Brush the grill grates with oil to prevent sticking.

Grill the chicken kabobs for about 10-15 minutes, turning occasionally, or until the chicken is fully cooked and has a nice char.

During grilling, baste the kabobs with the reserved marinade for added flavor.

Once the chicken is cooked through and the vegetables are tender, remove the kabobs from the grill.

Let the Grilled Chicken Kabobs rest for a few minutes before serving.

Serve the kabobs on a platter and enjoy this delicious and flavorful grilled dish!

Grilled Chicken Kabobs are a fantastic and versatile dish that brings together the smoky goodness of grilled chicken with the vibrant flavors of marinated vegetables. The marinade infuses the chicken with a perfect blend of sweet, savory, and spicy notes, while the grilling process adds a delicious char. Customize the kabobs with your favorite vegetables, and you have a visually appealing and tasty meal perfect for outdoor gatherings, barbecues, or a delightful weeknight dinner.

Garlic Butter Grilled Shrimp

Ingredients:

- 1 pound large shrimp, peeled and deveined
- 3 tablespoons unsalted butter, melted
- 3 cloves garlic, minced
- 2 tablespoons fresh parsley, chopped
- 1 tablespoon olive oil
- 1 tablespoon lemon juice
- 1/2 teaspoon paprika
- Salt and pepper, to taste
- Wooden or metal skewers

Instructions:

If using wooden skewers, soak them in water for at least 30 minutes to prevent burning during grilling.

In a bowl, combine melted butter, minced garlic, chopped parsley, olive oil, lemon juice, paprika, salt, and pepper to create the marinade.

Thread the shrimp onto the skewers, piercing them through both the tail and the body.

Place the shrimp skewers in a shallow dish and brush them generously with the garlic butter marinade.

Marinate the shrimp for about 15-30 minutes in the refrigerator.

Preheat your grill to medium-high heat.

Grease the grill grates with a bit of oil to prevent sticking.

Grill the shrimp skewers for approximately 2-3 minutes per side, or until the shrimp are opaque and have grill marks.

During grilling, baste the shrimp with the remaining garlic butter marinade for added flavor.

Once the shrimp are fully cooked, remove them from the grill.

Serve the Garlic Butter Grilled Shrimp hot, garnished with additional chopped parsley and lemon wedges if desired.

Enjoy this quick and tasty grilled shrimp dish as an appetizer or a main course!

Garlic Butter Grilled Shrimp is a simple and flavorful dish that highlights the natural sweetness of shrimp with the rich taste of garlic and butter. The marinade infuses the shrimp with a savory and aromatic profile, while grilling adds a smoky and charred element. This recipe is perfect for a quick and delicious appetizer or a light main course, and it's a great addition to your summer barbecue or outdoor grilling menu.

Dutch Oven Pot Roast

Ingredients:

- 3 to 4 pounds chuck roast
- Salt and black pepper, to taste
- 2 tablespoons vegetable oil
- 1 large onion, chopped
- 3 cloves garlic, minced
- 4 carrots, peeled and cut into chunks
- 4 potatoes, peeled and cut into chunks
- 2 celery stalks, chopped
- 2 cups beef broth
- 1 cup red wine (or additional beef broth)
- 2 tablespoons tomato paste
- 2 teaspoons dried thyme
- 2 teaspoons dried rosemary
- 2 bay leaves

Instructions:

Preheat your oven to 325°F (163°C).
Pat the chuck roast dry with paper towels and season it generously with salt and black pepper.
Heat vegetable oil in a Dutch oven over medium-high heat.
Sear the chuck roast on all sides until browned. This helps to lock in flavor.
Remove the roast from the Dutch oven and set it aside.
In the same Dutch oven, add chopped onions and minced garlic. Sauté until softened.
Add tomato paste and cook for an additional 2 minutes.
Pour in red wine (or beef broth) to deglaze the pot, scraping up any browned bits from the bottom.
Return the seared roast to the Dutch oven.
Add carrots, potatoes, celery, dried thyme, dried rosemary, and bay leaves.
Pour beef broth over the ingredients, ensuring the roast and vegetables are mostly covered.
Bring the liquid to a simmer.
Cover the Dutch oven with a lid and transfer it to the preheated oven.
Bake for approximately 3 to 4 hours, or until the roast is fork-tender.

Check the pot roast periodically, adding more broth if needed.
Once done, remove the Dutch oven from the oven, and let the pot roast rest for a few minutes before slicing.
Serve the Dutch Oven Pot Roast with the vegetables and enjoy the rich, flavorful dish!

Dutch Oven Pot Roast is a comforting and hearty meal that's perfect for gatherings or a cozy family dinner. Slow-cooked in a Dutch oven, the chuck roast becomes tender and infused with the flavors of vegetables, herbs, and a savory broth. This classic recipe is versatile, allowing you to customize the vegetables and seasonings to suit your taste. Serve the pot roast with crusty bread or over mashed potatoes for a satisfying and wholesome meal.

Campfire Baked Beans

Ingredients:

- 2 cans (15 ounces each) of your favorite baked beans
- 1/2 cup barbecue sauce
- 1/4 cup brown sugar
- 1/4 cup ketchup
- 1 tablespoon Dijon mustard
- 1 small onion, finely chopped
- 4 slices bacon, cooked and crumbled
- Salt and black pepper, to taste

Instructions:

Prepare your campfire with a medium heat level, ensuring you have a bed of hot coals.
In a cast-iron skillet or a campfire-friendly pot, combine the baked beans, barbecue sauce, brown sugar, ketchup, Dijon mustard, chopped onion, and crumbled bacon.
Stir the ingredients well to combine.
Place the skillet or pot on a grate over the campfire or directly on the hot coals.
Cook the Campfire Baked Beans for approximately 15-20 minutes, stirring occasionally, until the beans are hot and the flavors meld together.
Season with salt and black pepper to taste.
If the beans start to dry out, you can add a little water or broth to reach your desired consistency.
Once the beans are heated through and have a thick, saucy consistency, remove the skillet or pot from the campfire.
Let the Campfire Baked Beans rest for a few minutes before serving.
Serve the beans as a flavorful side dish to your campfire meals.

Campfire Baked Beans are a classic and delicious side dish that adds hearty flavor to your outdoor cooking experience. The combination of baked beans, barbecue sauce, brown sugar, and bacon creates a sweet and savory profile that's sure to be a hit around the campfire. This recipe is easy to make and can be customized with additional ingredients like chopped bell peppers, jalapeños, or ground meat for extra flair. Enjoy these Campfire Baked Beans alongside grilled meats or as a standalone dish during your camping adventures.

Caprese Salad Skewers

Ingredients:

- Cherry tomatoes
- Fresh mozzarella balls (bocconcini)
- Fresh basil leaves
- Balsamic glaze
- Olive oil
- Salt and black pepper, to taste
- Wooden skewers

Instructions:

Rinse the cherry tomatoes and basil leaves.
Thread a cherry tomato onto a wooden skewer, followed by a fresh basil leaf and a mozzarella ball. Repeat this pattern until the skewer is filled, leaving a small space at each end.
Arrange the Caprese Salad Skewers on a serving platter.
Drizzle balsamic glaze and olive oil over the skewers.
Sprinkle with salt and black pepper to taste.
Serve immediately and enjoy this refreshing and delightful appetizer!

Caprese Salad Skewers are a simple and elegant way to enjoy the classic flavors of a Caprese salad in a bite-sized form. The combination of sweet cherry tomatoes, creamy mozzarella, and aromatic basil, drizzled with balsamic glaze and olive oil, creates a burst of freshness with every bite. These skewers make for a perfect appetizer for parties, gatherings, or any occasion where you want to impress with a visually appealing and delicious dish.

Foil Packet Chicken Fajita Bowls

Ingredients:

- 1 pound boneless, skinless chicken breasts, thinly sliced
- 1 bell pepper, thinly sliced
- 1 onion, thinly sliced
- 1 cup cherry tomatoes, halved
- 1 tablespoon olive oil
- 1 packet (1.25 ounces) fajita seasoning mix
- Salt and black pepper, to taste
- Cooked rice or cauliflower rice (for serving)
- Optional toppings: shredded cheese, sour cream, guacamole, chopped cilantro

Instructions:

Preheat your oven to 425°F (218°C).
In a large bowl, combine the sliced chicken, bell pepper, onion, and cherry tomatoes.
Drizzle olive oil over the mixture and sprinkle the fajita seasoning, salt, and black pepper. Toss everything until well coated.
Cut four large squares of heavy-duty aluminum foil.
Divide the chicken and vegetable mixture evenly among the foil squares, placing it in the center of each.
Fold the foil over the ingredients, creating a packet. Seal the edges tightly.
Place the foil packets on a baking sheet and bake in the preheated oven for 20-25 minutes, or until the chicken is cooked through and the vegetables are tender.
Carefully open the foil packets, allowing steam to escape.
Serve the Foil Packet Chicken Fajita Bowls over cooked rice or cauliflower rice. Add optional toppings like shredded cheese, sour cream, guacamole, and chopped cilantro.
Enjoy this easy and flavorful meal with minimal cleanup!

Foil Packet Chicken Fajita Bowls are a convenient and delicious way to enjoy the bold flavors of chicken fajitas without the need for a skillet. The foil packets lock in moisture, creating juicy and tender chicken along with perfectly cooked vegetables. Customize your fajita bowls with your favorite toppings and enjoy a hassle-free, flavorful dinner that's perfect for busy weeknights or outdoor grilling adventures.

Cinnamon Sugar Campfire Donuts

Ingredients:

- 1 can refrigerated biscuit dough
- 1/2 cup granulated sugar
- 1 tablespoon ground cinnamon
- Vegetable oil (for frying)

Instructions:

In a bowl, combine granulated sugar and ground cinnamon. Set aside.

Heat vegetable oil in a deep skillet or pot over the campfire or on a camp stove. The oil should be approximately 350°F (180°C).

While the oil is heating, separate the biscuit dough and cut a hole in the center of each biscuit using a small round cutter or the cap of a water bottle.

Combine the donut holes with the donuts or fry them separately.

Carefully place the biscuits, a few at a time, into the hot oil. Fry until golden brown on one side, then flip them over using tongs to cook the other side. This usually takes about 1-2 minutes per side.

Once the donuts are golden brown on both sides, remove them from the oil using a slotted spoon and drain excess oil by placing them on a paper towel.

While the donuts are still warm, roll them in the cinnamon sugar mixture until well coated.

Serve the Cinnamon Sugar Campfire Donuts immediately and enjoy this sweet and satisfying treat!

Cinnamon Sugar Campfire Donuts are a delightful and easy-to-make camping treat. Using refrigerated biscuit dough makes the process quick and convenient, and frying them over a campfire adds a rustic and fun element to the cooking experience. Coated in a generous layer of cinnamon sugar, these campfire donuts are crispy on the outside and soft on the inside. They're perfect for breakfast, dessert, or a sweet snack while enjoying the great outdoors.

Grilled Portobello Mushrooms

Ingredients:

- 4 large Portobello mushrooms
- 3 tablespoons balsamic vinegar
- 2 tablespoons olive oil
- 2 cloves garlic, minced
- 1 teaspoon dried thyme
- Salt and black pepper, to taste
- Fresh parsley, chopped (for garnish)

Instructions:

Clean the Portobello mushrooms by gently wiping them with a damp cloth or brushing off any dirt. Remove the stems.
In a small bowl, whisk together balsamic vinegar, olive oil, minced garlic, dried thyme, salt, and black pepper to create the marinade.
Place the Portobello mushrooms in a shallow dish, gill side up. Pour the marinade over the mushrooms, ensuring they are well coated. Let them marinate for about 15-30 minutes.
Preheat your grill to medium heat.
Place the marinated Portobello mushrooms on the grill, gill side down.
Grill for approximately 4-5 minutes per side or until the mushrooms are tender and have grill marks.
During grilling, baste the mushrooms with any remaining marinade for added flavor.
Once the mushrooms are cooked to your liking, remove them from the grill.
Sprinkle chopped fresh parsley over the grilled Portobello mushrooms for garnish.
Serve the mushrooms as a side dish, on top of salads, in sandwiches, or as a flavorful meatless main course.
Enjoy these Grilled Portobello Mushrooms as a tasty and versatile addition to your summer grilling repertoire!

Grilled Portobello Mushrooms are a simple and delicious dish that showcases the earthy flavor of Portobello mushrooms enhanced by a savory balsamic marinade. The grilling process adds a smoky element and a satisfying texture to the mushrooms. Whether served as a side dish, on a salad, in a sandwich, or as a meatless main course, these grilled mushrooms are a versatile and flavorful option for vegetarians and mushroom enthusiasts alike.

Campfire Paella

Ingredients:

- 1 cup paella rice (Bomba or Arborio)
- 2 tablespoons olive oil
- 1 onion, finely chopped
- 2 cloves garlic, minced
- 1 red bell pepper, sliced
- 1 yellow bell pepper, sliced
- 1 teaspoon smoked paprika
- 1 teaspoon saffron threads (optional)
- 1/2 teaspoon turmeric powder (for color)
- 1 teaspoon paprika
- 1/2 teaspoon cayenne pepper (adjust to taste)
- 1/2 cup white wine
- 3 cups chicken or vegetable broth, hot
- 1 cup cherry tomatoes, halved
- 1 cup frozen peas
- 1 pound mixed seafood (shrimp, mussels, squid, etc.)
- Salt and black pepper, to taste
- Lemon wedges, for serving
- Fresh parsley, chopped (for garnish)

Instructions:

Heat the olive oil in a large, flat-bottomed pan or paella pan over a campfire or camp stove.

Add the chopped onion and sauté until softened.

Stir in the minced garlic and cook for an additional 1-2 minutes until fragrant.

Add the sliced bell peppers and cook until they begin to soften.

Sprinkle the smoked paprika, saffron threads (if using), turmeric powder, paprika, and cayenne pepper over the vegetables. Stir to combine.

Add the paella rice to the pan, stirring to coat the rice with the spices.

Pour in the white wine and cook for a couple of minutes to allow the alcohol to evaporate.

Begin adding the hot chicken or vegetable broth one ladle at a time, allowing the rice to absorb the liquid before adding more. Stir occasionally.

After about 10-15 minutes, add the cherry tomatoes, frozen peas, and mixed seafood to the paella. Continue adding broth as needed.
Season with salt and black pepper to taste.
Cook until the rice is tender, and the seafood is cooked through, usually around 20-25 minutes.
Once done, remove the Campfire Paella from the heat.
Garnish with chopped fresh parsley and serve with lemon wedges.
Enjoy this flavorful and satisfying Campfire Paella outdoors with friends and family!

Campfire Paella is a delicious and hearty one-pan meal that brings the rich flavors of traditional paella to the great outdoors. This recipe is perfect for camping or outdoor gatherings, allowing you to enjoy the essence of paella with a smoky campfire twist. The combination of aromatic spices, vibrant vegetables, and a mix of seafood creates a delightful dish that's sure to be a crowd-pleaser around the campfire.

Sausage and Egg Breakfast Sandwiches

Ingredients:

- 4 English muffins, split and toasted
- 4 pork sausage patties or links
- 4 large eggs
- Salt and black pepper, to taste
- 4 slices of cheese (cheddar, American, or your preference)
- Butter (for toasting and cooking)
- Optional toppings: ketchup, hot sauce, or mayo

Instructions:

Heat a skillet over medium heat and cook the sausage patties according to the package instructions. If using links, you can cut them in half or leave them whole. In the same skillet, melt a little butter and crack the eggs into the pan. Season with salt and black pepper. Cook the eggs to your preference (fried, scrambled, or as a folded omelet).
While the eggs are cooking, place a slice of cheese on each sausage patty to melt.
Once the eggs are cooked, assemble the sandwiches. Place a sausage patty with melted cheese on the bottom half of each English muffin.
Top the sausage with the cooked egg.
Add your preferred optional toppings, such as ketchup, hot sauce, or mayo.
Place the other half of the toasted English muffin on top to complete the sandwich.
Optional: Wrap the sandwiches in foil and warm them on a campfire grate for a minute or two to enhance the toasty goodness.
Serve the Sausage and Egg Breakfast Sandwiches warm and enjoy a hearty breakfast on the go!

These Sausage and Egg Breakfast Sandwiches are a satisfying and portable breakfast option, perfect for camping or busy mornings. The combination of savory sausage, melty cheese, and a perfectly cooked egg nestled between toasted English muffins creates a delicious and filling meal. Customize the sandwiches with your favorite toppings and enjoy a convenient and tasty breakfast that can be prepared easily, whether at home or around the campfire.

BBQ Chicken Foil Packets

Ingredients:

- 4 boneless, skinless chicken breasts
- 2 cups baby potatoes, halved
- 1 cup baby carrots
- 1 cup green beans, trimmed
- 1 cup barbecue sauce
- 4 cloves garlic, minced
- 2 tablespoons olive oil
- 1 teaspoon smoked paprika
- Salt and black pepper, to taste
- Fresh parsley, chopped (for garnish)

Instructions:

Preheat your grill to medium-high heat.
In a bowl, whisk together barbecue sauce, minced garlic, olive oil, smoked paprika, salt, and black pepper to create the barbecue sauce mixture.
Cut four large squares of heavy-duty aluminum foil.
Place a chicken breast in the center of each foil square.
Divide the baby potatoes, baby carrots, and green beans evenly among the foil packets, arranging them around the chicken.
Spoon the barbecue sauce mixture over each chicken breast and the vegetables, ensuring everything is well coated.
Fold the foil over the ingredients, creating a packet. Seal the edges tightly.
Place the foil packets on the preheated grill and cook for about 20-25 minutes or until the chicken is cooked through and the vegetables are tender.
Carefully open the foil packets, allowing steam to escape.
Garnish with chopped fresh parsley.
Serve the BBQ Chicken Foil Packets directly from the foil for an easy and flavorful meal with minimal cleanup.
Enjoy this delicious and hassle-free barbecue chicken with vegetables!

BBQ Chicken Foil Packets are a convenient and tasty way to enjoy a barbecue feast without a lot of cleanup. The combination of juicy barbecue chicken, baby potatoes, carrots, and green beans cooked in individual foil packets creates a flavorful and well-balanced meal. The foil packets also help to lock in the flavors, making the chicken and vegetables tender and infused with the delicious barbecue sauce. Whether you're grilling at home or enjoying the great outdoors, these foil packets are a crowd-pleaser that's easy to prepare and enjoy.

Dutch Oven Chicken and Rice

Ingredients:

- 4 bone-in, skin-on chicken thighs
- 1 cup long-grain white rice
- 1 onion, finely chopped
- 2 cloves garlic, minced
- 1 red bell pepper, diced
- 1 yellow bell pepper, diced
- 1 can (14 ounces) diced tomatoes, undrained
- 2 cups chicken broth
- 1 teaspoon paprika
- 1 teaspoon dried thyme
- Salt and black pepper, to taste
- Fresh parsley, chopped (for garnish)

Instructions:

Preheat your Dutch oven over medium heat.
Season the chicken thighs with salt, black pepper, and paprika.
Place the chicken thighs, skin side down, in the preheated Dutch oven. Brown them on both sides until the skin is crispy. Remove and set aside.
In the same Dutch oven, sauté the chopped onion and minced garlic until softened.
Add the diced red and yellow bell peppers, cooking for an additional 2-3 minutes.
Stir in the long-grain white rice, allowing it to toast for about 2 minutes.
Pour in the diced tomatoes with their juice and add the chicken broth. Stir to combine.
Nestle the browned chicken thighs back into the rice mixture, skin side up.
Sprinkle dried thyme over the chicken and rice.
Cover the Dutch oven with a lid and simmer over low heat for approximately 25-30 minutes or until the chicken is cooked through, and the rice has absorbed the liquid.
Check the seasoning and adjust with salt and black pepper if needed.
Garnish with chopped fresh parsley before serving.
Serve the Dutch Oven Chicken and Rice directly from the pot for a comforting and flavorful one-pot meal.

Enjoy this Dutch Oven Chicken and Rice, a delicious and hearty dish that brings together tender chicken, aromatic rice, and colorful vegetables in one pot. The Dutch oven allows for slow cooking, ensuring the flavors meld together, creating a satisfying and comforting meal. Whether you're cooking indoors or outdoors, this recipe is a versatile and convenient option for a wholesome dinner.

Grilled Halloumi Skewers

Ingredients:

- 1 block of halloumi cheese, cut into cubes
- Cherry tomatoes
- Red and yellow bell peppers, cut into chunks
- Red onion, cut into wedges
- Zucchini, sliced into rounds
- Olive oil
- Lemon juice
- Fresh oregano, chopped (or dried oregano)
- Salt and black pepper, to taste
- Wooden skewers, soaked in water

Instructions:

Preheat your grill to medium-high heat.
In a bowl, combine olive oil, lemon juice, chopped oregano, salt, and black pepper. This will be your marinade.
Thread the halloumi cheese cubes, cherry tomatoes, bell pepper chunks, red onion wedges, and zucchini rounds onto the soaked wooden skewers, alternating the ingredients.
Brush the skewers generously with the prepared marinade, coating all sides.
Place the skewers on the preheated grill and cook for about 2-3 minutes on each side or until the halloumi is golden brown and has grill marks.
While grilling, continue to brush the skewers with the marinade to keep them moist and flavorful.
Once the halloumi is grilled to your liking and the vegetables are tender, remove the skewers from the grill.
Garnish with additional chopped oregano if desired.
Serve the Grilled Halloumi Skewers hot, either as an appetizer or a delightful vegetarian main dish.

Grilled Halloumi Skewers are a tasty and easy-to-make dish that's perfect for summer grilling or any outdoor gathering. The halloumi cheese becomes wonderfully crispy on the outside while remaining soft and gooey on the inside. The combination of grilled halloumi with colorful vegetables and a zesty marinade creates a flavorful and satisfying dish. Enjoy these skewers as a light meal, appetizer, or side dish at your next barbecue or picnic!

Campfire Nachos

Ingredients:

- Tortilla chips
- 1 cup cooked and seasoned ground beef or shredded chicken
- 1 cup shredded cheddar cheese
- 1 cup shredded Monterey Jack cheese
- 1 cup black beans, drained and rinsed
- 1 cup corn kernels (fresh or canned)
- 1 cup diced tomatoes
- 1/2 cup sliced jalapeños (optional)
- 1/2 cup sliced black olives
- 1/4 cup chopped green onions
- Sour cream, guacamole, and salsa for serving

Instructions:

Prepare your campfire by building a medium-sized fire with glowing embers.
Assemble a sturdy aluminum foil packet by layering two large pieces of heavy-duty foil to create a durable base.
Arrange a layer of tortilla chips on the foil, creating an even base.
Sprinkle half of the seasoned ground beef or shredded chicken over the chips.
Add half of the shredded cheddar and Monterey Jack cheeses.
Distribute half of the black beans, corn, diced tomatoes, jalapeños (if using), black olives, and green onions evenly over the chips.
Repeat the layers by adding another round of tortilla chips and topping with the remaining ingredients.
Seal the foil packet tightly, ensuring that it's well-sealed on all sides.
Place the foil packet on a grate or directly onto the campfire embers, allowing it to cook for about 10-15 minutes or until the cheese is melted, and the nachos are heated through.
Carefully remove the foil packet from the fire using tongs or heat-resistant gloves.
Open the foil packet, and let everyone customize their nachos with sour cream, guacamole, and salsa.
Serve the Campfire Nachos directly from the foil for a fun and delicious outdoor snack.

Enjoy these Campfire Nachos as a flavorful and shareable treat during your camping adventures. The combination of melty cheese, seasoned meat, and vibrant toppings creates a satisfying and easy-to-make camping dish. Gather around the campfire, share a foil packet of nachos, and savor the goodness of this camping classic!

Dutch Oven Lemon Blueberry Cake

Ingredients:

- 2 cups all-purpose flour
- 1 cup granulated sugar
- 1 teaspoon baking powder
- 1/2 teaspoon baking soda
- 1/4 teaspoon salt
- 1/2 cup unsalted butter, softened
- 2 large eggs
- 1 cup plain Greek yogurt
- 1 teaspoon vanilla extract
- Zest of 1 lemon
- 2 cups fresh blueberries
- Powdered sugar (for dusting, optional)

Instructions:

Preheat your Dutch oven by placing hot charcoal briquettes on the lid and bottom to achieve a medium heat.
In a bowl, whisk together the flour, baking powder, baking soda, and salt. Set aside.
In another large bowl, cream together the softened butter and granulated sugar until light and fluffy.
Add the eggs one at a time, beating well after each addition.
Stir in the Greek yogurt, vanilla extract, and lemon zest until well combined.
Gradually add the dry ingredients to the wet ingredients, mixing until just combined.
Gently fold in the fresh blueberries, being careful not to overmix.
Grease the bottom and sides of the Dutch oven with butter or cooking spray.
Pour the batter into the prepared Dutch oven.
Place the lid on the Dutch oven and arrange hot charcoal briquettes on top of the lid.
Bake the cake in the Dutch oven for approximately 45-55 minutes or until a toothpick inserted into the center comes out clean.
Rotate the Dutch oven and the lid occasionally to ensure even baking.
Once the cake is done, remove it from the heat and let it cool in the Dutch oven.
Dust the top with powdered sugar if desired before serving.

Slice and enjoy this delicious Dutch Oven Lemon Blueberry Cake.

This Dutch Oven Lemon Blueberry Cake is a delightful dessert that can be easily prepared outdoors while camping. The combination of zesty lemon, juicy blueberries, and a tender cake texture makes it a perfect treat for any camping adventure. Enjoy the sweet aroma and flavors of this Dutch oven cake around the campfire with friends and family.

Foil Packet Chicken Parmesan

Ingredients:

- 4 boneless, skinless chicken breasts
- Salt and black pepper, to taste
- 1 cup marinara sauce
- 1 cup shredded mozzarella cheese
- 1/2 cup grated Parmesan cheese
- 1 teaspoon dried oregano
- 1 teaspoon dried basil
- 1/2 teaspoon garlic powder
- 1/4 teaspoon red pepper flakes (optional)
- Fresh basil or parsley, chopped (for garnish)
- Olive oil (for drizzling)

Instructions:

Preheat your oven to 425°F (220°C).
Season the chicken breasts with salt and black pepper on both sides.
Place each chicken breast on a large piece of heavy-duty aluminum foil.
Spoon a generous amount of marinara sauce over each chicken breast.
Sprinkle shredded mozzarella and grated Parmesan cheese over the top of each chicken breast.
Sprinkle dried oregano, dried basil, garlic powder, and red pepper flakes (if using) evenly over the cheese.
Drizzle a bit of olive oil over each chicken packet.
Fold the foil over the chicken, sealing the edges tightly to create individual packets.
Place the foil packets on a baking sheet and bake in the preheated oven for about 25-30 minutes or until the chicken is cooked through and the cheese is melted and bubbly.
Carefully open the foil packets, allowing steam to escape.
Garnish with chopped fresh basil or parsley.
Serve the Foil Packet Chicken Parmesan directly from the foil for a hassle-free and delicious meal.

Enjoy this easy-to-make Foil Packet Chicken Parmesan, a convenient way to prepare a classic Italian dish with minimal cleanup. The combination of juicy chicken, marinara sauce, and melted cheese creates a flavorful and satisfying meal. This foil packet method is versatile and perfect for busy weeknights or outdoor grilling. Customize the seasonings to your liking and savor the deliciousness of Chicken Parmesan in a convenient foil packet.

Campfire Tinfoil Packet Tacos

Ingredients:

- 1 pound ground beef or ground turkey
- 1 packet taco seasoning
- 1 cup cooked black beans, drained
- 1 cup corn kernels (fresh or canned)
- 1 cup diced tomatoes
- 1 cup shredded cheddar cheese
- 1/2 cup diced red onions
- 1/4 cup chopped fresh cilantro
- 8 small flour tortillas
- Sour cream, salsa, guacamole, and lime wedges for serving

Instructions:

Preheat your campfire or grill to medium-high heat.
In a large bowl, mix the ground beef or turkey with the taco seasoning until well combined.
Tear off 8 large squares of heavy-duty aluminum foil, each large enough to hold one serving.
Place a portion of the seasoned meat in the center of each foil square.
Top the meat with black beans, corn, diced tomatoes, shredded cheddar cheese, and diced red onions.
Fold the foil over the ingredients, creating a packet. Seal the edges tightly.
Place the foil packets on the campfire grate or grill and cook for about 15-20 minutes, flipping halfway through, until the meat is cooked through and the ingredients are heated.
Carefully open the foil packets, allowing steam to escape.
Warm the flour tortillas on the campfire grate or grill for a minute on each side.
Spoon the taco filling onto the warmed tortillas.
Garnish with chopped cilantro and serve with sour cream, salsa, guacamole, and lime wedges on the side.
Enjoy these delicious and easy-to-make Campfire Tinfoil Packet Tacos right at your campsite.

These Campfire Tinfoil Packet Tacos are a fun and convenient way to enjoy tacos while camping. The foil packets help to cook the ingredients together, creating a flavorful and mess-free camping meal. Customize the taco fillings to your liking and savor the delicious taste of tacos by the campfire. Whether you're camping or just craving an outdoor-inspired meal, these foil packet tacos are sure to be a hit!

Grilled Stuffed Portobello Mushrooms

Ingredients:

- 4 large portobello mushrooms, stems removed
- 1 tablespoon olive oil
- 2 cloves garlic, minced
- 1 cup spinach, chopped
- 1/2 cup sun-dried tomatoes, chopped
- 1/2 cup feta cheese, crumbled
- Salt and black pepper, to taste
- Fresh basil, chopped (for garnish)

Instructions:

   Preheat your grill to medium-high heat.
   Clean the portobello mushrooms and remove the stems.
   In a small skillet, heat olive oil over medium heat. Add minced garlic and sauté for about 1 minute until fragrant.
   Add chopped spinach to the skillet and cook until wilted.
   Remove the skillet from heat and stir in sun-dried tomatoes and crumbled feta cheese. Season with salt and black pepper to taste.
   Brush the outside of the portobello mushrooms with olive oil.
   Spoon the spinach, sun-dried tomato, and feta mixture into the mushroom caps.
   Place the stuffed mushrooms on the preheated grill and cook for about 8-10 minutes, or until the mushrooms are tender and the filling is heated through.
   Carefully remove the stuffed mushrooms from the grill.
   Garnish with chopped fresh basil.
   Serve the Grilled Stuffed Portobello Mushrooms as a flavorful and satisfying appetizer or side dish.

These Grilled Stuffed Portobello Mushrooms are a delicious and healthy option for a vegetarian or appetizer dish. The combination of savory spinach, sweet sun-dried tomatoes, and creamy feta cheese creates a flavorful filling for the meaty portobello mushrooms. Grilling adds a smoky flavor to the mushrooms, making them a delightful addition to your barbecue or outdoor gathering. Enjoy these stuffed mushrooms as a tasty and satisfying dish for any occasion!

Dutch Oven Chicken Pot Pie

Ingredients:

For the Filling:

- 2 tablespoons unsalted butter
- 1 onion, finely chopped
- 2 carrots, diced
- 2 celery stalks, diced
- 3 cloves garlic, minced
- 1/3 cup all-purpose flour
- 2 cups cooked chicken, shredded or diced
- 2 cups chicken broth
- 1 cup frozen peas
- 1 cup frozen corn
- 1 cup whole milk
- Salt and black pepper, to taste
- 1 teaspoon dried thyme
- 1 teaspoon dried parsley

For the Biscuit Topping:

- 2 cups all-purpose flour
- 1 tablespoon baking powder
- 1 teaspoon sugar
- 1/2 teaspoon salt
- 1/2 cup unsalted butter, cold and cut into small pieces
- 3/4 cup buttermilk

Instructions:

Preheat your Dutch oven by placing hot charcoal briquettes on the lid and bottom to achieve a medium heat.
For the filling: In the Dutch oven, melt butter over medium heat. Add chopped onion, diced carrots, and diced celery. Sauté until the vegetables are softened, about 5 minutes. Add minced garlic and cook for an additional minute.

Stir in the flour and cook for 1-2 minutes to eliminate the raw flour taste. Gradually add chicken broth and whole milk, stirring constantly to avoid lumps. Cook until the mixture thickens.

Add shredded or diced cooked chicken, frozen peas, frozen corn, dried thyme, dried parsley, salt, and black pepper. Stir to combine. Allow the filling to simmer for a few minutes until it reaches a thick consistency.

For the biscuit topping: In a separate bowl, whisk together flour, baking powder, sugar, and salt. Cut in cold butter using a pastry cutter or your fingers until the mixture resembles coarse crumbs. Add buttermilk and stir until just combined.

Drop spoonfuls of the biscuit dough onto the chicken filling in the Dutch oven.

Cover the Dutch oven with the lid and place additional hot charcoal briquettes on top of the lid.

Bake for about 25-30 minutes or until the biscuit topping is golden brown and cooked through.

Carefully remove the Dutch oven from the heat.

Serve the Dutch Oven Chicken Pot Pie directly from the pot, scooping out portions of the filling and biscuit topping.

Enjoy this comforting Dutch Oven Chicken Pot Pie as a hearty and delicious campfire meal. The combination of a savory chicken and vegetable filling with a golden-brown biscuit topping creates a flavorful and satisfying dish. Whether you're camping or cooking outdoors, this Dutch oven recipe is a classic comfort food that brings warmth and goodness to any gathering.

Foil Packet Lemon Garlic Asparagus

Ingredients:

- 1 bunch asparagus, trimmed
- 2 tablespoons olive oil
- 2 cloves garlic, minced
- Zest of 1 lemon
- 2 tablespoons fresh lemon juice
- Salt and black pepper, to taste
- Fresh parsley, chopped (for garnish)

Instructions:

Preheat your grill to medium-high heat.
Tear off a large piece of heavy-duty aluminum foil.
Place the trimmed asparagus in the center of the foil.
In a small bowl, whisk together olive oil, minced garlic, lemon zest, and lemon juice.
Drizzle the lemon garlic mixture over the asparagus.
Season the asparagus with salt and black pepper to taste.
Fold the foil over the asparagus, creating a packet. Seal the edges tightly.
Place the foil packet on the preheated grill and cook for about 10-15 minutes, or until the asparagus is tender-crisp.
Carefully open the foil packet, allowing steam to escape.
Garnish the asparagus with chopped fresh parsley.
Serve the Foil Packet Lemon Garlic Asparagus as a flavorful and vibrant side dish.

Enjoy this quick and easy Foil Packet Lemon Garlic Asparagus as a delicious side dish for your outdoor grilling. The combination of fresh asparagus, zesty lemon, and savory garlic creates a tasty and vibrant flavor profile. The foil packet method allows the asparagus to steam and absorb the delicious flavors, resulting in tender-crisp and flavorful spears. Add this simple and healthy recipe to your outdoor cooking repertoire for a delightful side dish that complements any meal.

Campfire Banana Boats

Ingredients:

- Bananas (1 per serving)
- Chocolate chips
- Mini marshmallows
- Other optional toppings: chopped nuts, shredded coconut, caramel sauce

Instructions:

Preheat your campfire to medium-high heat.
Leave the banana peel on and make a lengthwise cut through the top, splitting the banana in half (but not cutting all the way through).
Create a small well in the center of the banana halves.
Fill the well with chocolate chips, mini marshmallows, and any other toppings you desire.
Wrap the banana in aluminum foil, leaving the top exposed.
Place the foil-wrapped bananas on the campfire grate and cook for about 5-10 minutes, or until the chocolate and marshmallows are melted and gooey.
Carefully remove the banana boats from the campfire.
Open the foil, and use a spoon to scoop out the delicious melty goodness.
Enjoy your Campfire Banana Boats straight from the peel!

Campfire Banana Boats are a simple and delightful campfire treat that combines the sweetness of bananas with gooey chocolate and marshmallows. The foil wrapping helps to contain the mess and allows the ingredients to melt together, creating a warm and satisfying dessert. Feel free to customize with your favorite toppings for a personalized and delicious campfire experience.

Shrimp and Sausage Foil Packets

Ingredients:

- 1 pound large shrimp, peeled and deveined
- 1 pound smoked sausage, sliced into rounds
- 1 pound baby potatoes, halved
- 2 ears of corn, each cut into 4 pieces
- 1 bell pepper, sliced
- 1 onion, sliced
- 4 cloves garlic, minced
- 1/4 cup olive oil
- 2 tablespoons Cajun seasoning
- Salt and black pepper, to taste
- Fresh parsley, chopped (for garnish)
- Lemon wedges (for serving)

Instructions:

Preheat your grill to medium-high heat.
In a large bowl, combine the shrimp, smoked sausage, baby potatoes, corn pieces, bell pepper slices, and onion slices.
In a small bowl, whisk together the olive oil, minced garlic, Cajun seasoning, salt, and black pepper.
Pour the olive oil mixture over the shrimp and sausage mixture. Toss until everything is well coated.
Tear off large pieces of heavy-duty aluminum foil.
Divide the mixture among the foil pieces, placing a portion in the center of each piece.
Fold the foil over the ingredients, creating a packet. Seal the edges tightly.
Place the foil packets on the preheated grill and cook for about 20-25 minutes, or until the shrimp are opaque, the sausage is heated through, and the potatoes are tender.
Carefully open the foil packets, allowing steam to escape.
Garnish with chopped fresh parsley.
Serve the Shrimp and Sausage Foil Packets immediately, with lemon wedges on the side.

Enjoy this Shrimp and Sausage Foil Packets recipe for a delicious and hassle-free meal cooked on the grill. The combination of juicy shrimp, smoky sausage, and a variety of colorful vegetables creates a flavorful and satisfying dish. The Cajun seasoning adds a spicy kick to the mix, making it a perfect option for a quick and tasty outdoor meal.

Grilled Caesar Salad

Ingredients:

For the Dressing:

- 1/2 cup mayonnaise
- 1/4 cup grated Parmesan cheese
- 2 tablespoons lemon juice
- 1 tablespoon Dijon mustard
- 2 cloves garlic, minced
- Salt and black pepper, to taste

For the Salad:

- Romaine lettuce hearts, halved lengthwise
- Olive oil, for brushing
- Croutons (store-bought or homemade)
- Grated Parmesan cheese, for garnish
- Lemon wedges, for serving

Instructions:

Preheat your grill to medium-high heat.
In a bowl, whisk together mayonnaise, grated Parmesan cheese, lemon juice, Dijon mustard, minced garlic, salt, and black pepper to make the dressing. Adjust the seasoning to taste.
Brush the cut sides of the Romaine lettuce hearts with olive oil.
Place the lettuce halves on the preheated grill, cut side down. Grill for about 1-2 minutes, or until the edges are charred and the lettuce has a smoky flavor.
Remove the grilled lettuce from the grill and place on serving plates.
Drizzle the Caesar dressing over the grilled Romaine halves.
Top the salads with croutons and sprinkle with additional grated Parmesan cheese.
Serve the Grilled Caesar Salad with lemon wedges on the side.

Enjoy this unique twist on a classic Caesar Salad with the added flavor of grilling. The charred Romaine lettuce adds a smoky element, while the homemade Caesar dressing provides a creamy and tangy finish. This Grilled Caesar Salad makes for a refreshing and flavorful side dish or a light main course for your outdoor grilling gatherings.

Dutch Oven Pumpkin Bread

Ingredients:

- 2 cups all-purpose flour
- 1 teaspoon baking powder
- 1/2 teaspoon baking soda
- 1/2 teaspoon salt
- 1 teaspoon ground cinnamon
- 1/2 teaspoon ground nutmeg
- 1/4 teaspoon ground cloves
- 1/4 teaspoon ground ginger
- 1/2 cup unsalted butter, softened
- 1 cup granulated sugar
- 2 large eggs
- 1 cup canned pumpkin puree
- 1 teaspoon vanilla extract
- 1/2 cup buttermilk

Instructions:

Preheat your Dutch oven by placing hot charcoal briquettes on the lid and bottom to achieve a medium heat.
In a medium bowl, whisk together the flour, baking powder, baking soda, salt, cinnamon, nutmeg, cloves, and ginger. Set aside.
In a large bowl, cream together the softened butter and granulated sugar until light and fluffy.
Add the eggs one at a time, beating well after each addition.
Stir in the pumpkin puree and vanilla extract until well combined.
Gradually add the dry ingredients to the wet ingredients, alternating with the buttermilk. Begin and end with the dry ingredients, mixing until just combined.
Grease the inside of the Dutch oven with butter or cooking spray.
Pour the pumpkin bread batter into the greased Dutch oven, spreading it evenly.
Place the lid on the Dutch oven and arrange hot charcoal briquettes on top of the lid.
Bake for about 45-50 minutes, or until a toothpick inserted into the center of the bread comes out clean.

Carefully remove the Dutch oven from the heat and let the pumpkin bread cool before slicing.
Serve slices of Dutch Oven Pumpkin Bread and enjoy!

This Dutch Oven Pumpkin Bread is a delicious and comforting treat, perfect for outdoor cooking or camping adventures. The combination of warm spices and pumpkin creates a flavorful bread that's moist and satisfying. Baking in a Dutch oven over charcoal imparts a rustic charm and enhances the overall experience. Enjoy this pumpkin bread as a delightful dessert or breakfast option during your outdoor gatherings.

Foil Packet Teriyaki Salmon

Ingredients:

- 4 salmon fillets
- 1/2 cup teriyaki sauce
- 2 tablespoons soy sauce
- 2 tablespoons honey
- 2 cloves garlic, minced
- 1 tablespoon fresh ginger, grated
- 1 tablespoon sesame oil
- 1 bunch asparagus, trimmed
- 1 red bell pepper, thinly sliced
- Sesame seeds and chopped green onions (for garnish)
- Cooked rice (for serving)

Instructions:

Preheat your grill to medium-high heat.
In a bowl, whisk together teriyaki sauce, soy sauce, honey, minced garlic, grated ginger, and sesame oil to create the teriyaki marinade.
Place each salmon fillet on a separate piece of heavy-duty aluminum foil.
Pour the teriyaki marinade over the salmon fillets, ensuring they are well coated.
Arrange trimmed asparagus and sliced red bell pepper around each salmon fillet.
Fold the foil over the ingredients, creating individual packets. Seal the edges tightly.
Place the foil packets on the preheated grill and cook for about 12-15 minutes, or until the salmon is cooked through and flakes easily with a fork.
Carefully open the foil packets, allowing steam to escape.
Garnish the teriyaki salmon with sesame seeds and chopped green onions.
Serve the salmon over cooked rice.

Enjoy this Foil Packet Teriyaki Salmon for a quick, easy, and flavorful grilled meal. The teriyaki marinade infuses the salmon with a sweet and savory taste, while the foil packet method ensures the fish stays moist and flavorful. The addition of asparagus and red bell pepper creates a well-balanced and colorful dish. Serve it over rice for a complete and satisfying meal that's perfect for outdoor dining.

Campfire TInfoil Packet Bruschetta Chicken

Ingredients:

- 4 boneless, skinless chicken breasts
- 2 cups cherry tomatoes, halved
- 1/2 cup fresh basil, chopped
- 4 cloves garlic, minced
- 1/4 cup balsamic glaze
- 1/4 cup shredded mozzarella cheese
- Salt and black pepper, to taste
- Olive oil, for drizzling
- Fresh basil leaves (for garnish)

Instructions:

Preheat your campfire or grill to medium-high heat.
Lay out four large pieces of heavy-duty aluminum foil.
Place a chicken breast in the center of each piece of foil.
In a bowl, combine the cherry tomatoes, chopped fresh basil, minced garlic, balsamic glaze, and shredded mozzarella cheese. Mix well.
Spoon the bruschetta mixture over each chicken breast.
Season the chicken with salt and black pepper to taste.
Drizzle a bit of olive oil over each chicken breast.
Fold the foil over the ingredients, creating individual packets. Seal the edges tightly.
Place the foil packets on the campfire grate or grill and cook for about 20-25 minutes, or until the chicken is cooked through.
Carefully open the foil packets, allowing steam to escape.
Garnish with fresh basil leaves.
Serve the Bruschetta Chicken over pasta, rice, or with a side of crusty bread.

Enjoy this delicious and easy Campfire Tin Foil Packet Bruschetta Chicken for a flavorful outdoor dining experience. The combination of juicy chicken, fresh tomatoes, basil, and balsamic glaze creates a tasty and satisfying dish. The foil packet method ensures the chicken stays moist and cooks evenly over the campfire or grill. Serve it with your favorite side for a complete and enjoyable camping or outdoor meal.

Dutch Oven S'mores Cake

Ingredients:

- 2 cups graham cracker crumbs
- 1/2 cup unsalted butter, melted
- 1 package (18.25 ounces) chocolate cake mix
- Ingredients required for the cake mix (eggs, water, oil)
- 2 cups mini marshmallows
- 1 cup chocolate chips
- 1 cup crushed graham crackers
- 1/2 cup milk chocolate, melted (optional, for drizzling)

Instructions:

Preheat your Dutch oven by placing hot charcoal briquettes on the lid and bottom to achieve a medium heat.
In a bowl, combine graham cracker crumbs with melted butter to create the crust mixture.
Press the graham cracker mixture into the bottom of the Dutch oven to form an even crust.
Prepare the chocolate cake mix according to the package instructions.
Pour the cake batter over the graham cracker crust in the Dutch oven.
Sprinkle mini marshmallows, chocolate chips, and crushed graham crackers evenly over the cake batter.
Place the lid on the Dutch oven and arrange hot charcoal briquettes on top.
Bake for about 25-30 minutes, or until a toothpick inserted into the center of the cake comes out clean.
Carefully remove the Dutch oven from the heat.
If desired, drizzle melted milk chocolate over the top of the cake.
Let the S'mores Cake cool slightly before serving.
Scoop out portions and enjoy your Dutch Oven S'mores Cake!

This Dutch Oven S'mores Cake is a delightful camping treat that combines the classic flavors of s'mores with the convenience of a cake. The graham cracker crust, chocolate cake, marshmallows, and additional toppings create a delicious and gooey dessert that's perfect for outdoor gatherings. The Dutch oven method allows you to enjoy a warm and comforting S'mores Cake while camping or cooking over an open fire.

Grilled Zucchini Ribbon Salad

Ingredients:

- 4 medium-sized zucchini
- 2 tablespoons olive oil
- Salt and black pepper, to taste
- 1/4 cup pine nuts, toasted
- 1/4 cup feta cheese, crumbled
- 1/4 cup fresh basil, thinly sliced
- 1 tablespoon balsamic glaze (for drizzling)

Instructions:

Preheat your grill to medium-high heat.
Trim the ends of the zucchini and, using a vegetable peeler or a mandoline, slice the zucchini into thin ribbons.
In a bowl, toss the zucchini ribbons with olive oil, salt, and black pepper until well coated.
Place the zucchini ribbons on the preheated grill grates and cook for 1-2 minutes per side, just until grill marks appear. Be careful not to overcook; you want the zucchini to remain tender.
Remove the grilled zucchini ribbons from the grill and let them cool slightly.
Arrange the grilled zucchini ribbons on a serving platter.
Sprinkle toasted pine nuts, crumbled feta cheese, and thinly sliced fresh basil over the zucchini ribbons.
Drizzle balsamic glaze over the salad.
Serve the Grilled Zucchini Ribbon Salad immediately as a refreshing and flavorful side dish.

This Grilled Zucchini Ribbon Salad is a light and delicious side dish that showcases the natural flavors of zucchini with a hint of smokiness from the grill. The combination of grilled zucchini, toasted pine nuts, feta cheese, and fresh basil creates a well-balanced and satisfying salad. Drizzling with balsamic glaze adds a touch of sweetness and acidity. Enjoy this salad as a refreshing addition to your summer meals or as a side dish for grilled meats and seafood.

Campfire Biscuits and Gravy

Ingredients:

For the Biscuits:

- 2 cups all-purpose flour
- 1 tablespoon baking powder
- 1 teaspoon salt
- 1/2 cup unsalted butter, cold and cubed
- 3/4 cup milk

For the Gravy:

- 1 pound breakfast sausage (pork or turkey)
- 1/4 cup all-purpose flour
- 3 cups milk
- Salt and black pepper, to taste

Instructions:

Biscuits:

In a large mixing bowl, whisk together the flour, baking powder, and salt.
Add the cold, cubed butter to the flour mixture. Use a pastry cutter or your fingers to cut the butter into the flour until the mixture resembles coarse crumbs.
Pour in the milk and stir until just combined. Do not overmix.
Turn the dough out onto a floured surface and gently knead it a few times until it comes together.
Roll out the dough to about 1/2-inch thickness.
Use a round biscuit cutter to cut out biscuits and place them on a parchment paper-lined plate.
Preheat your campfire or grill.
Place a cast-iron skillet on the campfire grate or grill grates to heat.
Once the skillet is hot, place the biscuits in the skillet, close to each other but not touching.
Cover the skillet with a lid or foil and cook for about 15-20 minutes, turning the biscuits occasionally, until they are golden brown and cooked through.

Gravy:

In a separate cast-iron skillet or Dutch oven, cook the breakfast sausage over the campfire or grill until browned and cooked through.

Sprinkle flour over the cooked sausage, stirring to combine and cook for 1-2 minutes to remove the raw flour taste.

Slowly pour in the milk, stirring continuously to avoid lumps.

Cook the gravy over the campfire, stirring frequently, until it thickens to your desired consistency.

Season the gravy with salt and black pepper to taste.

Assembly:

Split the biscuits in half and place them on serving plates.

Spoon the hot sausage gravy over the biscuits.

Serve the Campfire Biscuits and Gravy immediately and enjoy your delicious campfire breakfast!

This Campfire Biscuits and Gravy recipe brings the comfort of a classic breakfast to your outdoor cooking experience. The biscuits are made from scratch and cooked over the campfire, while the savory sausage gravy is prepared in a separate skillet. It's a hearty and satisfying meal perfect for camping or any outdoor adventure.

Dutch Oven Peach Cobbler

Ingredients:

For the Peach Filling:

- 6 cups fresh or canned peaches, sliced
- 1 cup granulated sugar
- 1 tablespoon lemon juice
- 1 teaspoon vanilla extract
- 2 tablespoons cornstarch

For the Cobbler Topping:

- 1 cup all-purpose flour
- 1 cup granulated sugar
- 1 teaspoon baking powder
- 1/2 teaspoon salt
- 1 cup milk
- 1/2 cup unsalted butter, melted

Instructions:

Preheat your campfire or grill for medium heat.
In a large mixing bowl, combine the sliced peaches, granulated sugar, lemon juice, vanilla extract, and cornstarch. Toss until the peaches are evenly coated.
Pour the peach mixture into a well-seasoned 12-inch cast-iron Dutch oven.
In another bowl, whisk together the flour, granulated sugar, baking powder, and salt for the cobbler topping.
Add the milk to the dry ingredients and stir until just combined.
Pour the melted butter into the batter and mix until smooth.
Spoon the cobbler batter over the peaches in the Dutch oven, spreading it evenly.
Place the lid on the Dutch oven and set it on the campfire grate or grill grates.
Arrange hot charcoal briquettes on the lid of the Dutch oven to create an even temperature.
Bake the peach cobbler for about 40-45 minutes or until the cobbler topping is golden brown and cooked through.

Carefully remove the Dutch oven from the heat.
Allow the peach cobbler to cool for a few minutes before serving.
Scoop the warm Dutch Oven Peach Cobbler into bowls and enjoy with a scoop of vanilla ice cream, if desired.

This Dutch Oven Peach Cobbler is a classic camping dessert that captures the sweet and juicy flavors of fresh peaches in a warm and comforting cobbler. The combination of a gooey peach filling and a golden brown cobbler topping creates a delicious treat perfect for outdoor gatherings. Serve it with a scoop of vanilla ice cream for an extra indulgent camping dessert experience.

Foil Packet Teriyaki Veggie Bowls

Ingredients:

- 2 cups broccoli florets
- 1 red bell pepper, thinly sliced
- 1 yellow bell pepper, thinly sliced
- 1 zucchini, thinly sliced
- 1 carrot, thinly sliced or julienned
- 1 cup snap peas, ends trimmed
- 1/2 cup teriyaki sauce
- 2 tablespoons soy sauce
- 2 tablespoons honey
- 1 tablespoon sesame oil
- 1 teaspoon grated ginger
- 1 teaspoon minced garlic
- Cooked rice, for serving
- Sesame seeds and green onions, for garnish

Instructions:

Preheat your grill or campfire to medium-high heat.
In a bowl, whisk together the teriyaki sauce, soy sauce, honey, sesame oil, grated ginger, and minced garlic to create the teriyaki sauce.
Tear off large pieces of heavy-duty aluminum foil for each foil packet.
Divide the broccoli, red bell pepper, yellow bell pepper, zucchini, carrot, and snap peas among the foil pieces.
Drizzle the teriyaki sauce over the veggies in each foil packet.
Fold the foil over the veggies, sealing the edges tightly to create packets.
Place the foil packets on the grill grates or campfire grate.
Cook for about 15-20 minutes, turning once, or until the veggies are tender.
Carefully open the foil packets, allowing steam to escape.
Serve the Teriyaki Veggie Bowls over cooked rice.
Garnish with sesame seeds and chopped green onions.
Enjoy these delicious and flavorful Foil Packet Teriyaki Veggie Bowls for a quick and easy camping meal!

These Foil Packet Teriyaki Veggie Bowls are a convenient and tasty way to enjoy a variety of vegetables with a delicious teriyaki sauce. The foil packets help steam the veggies to perfection, and the teriyaki sauce adds a sweet and savory flavor. Serve over cooked rice for a complete and satisfying camping meal. Customize the veggies based on your preferences for a personalized and nutritious outdoor dining experience.

www.ingramcontent.com/pod-product-compliance
Lightning Source LLC
LaVergne TN
LVHW081609060526
838201LV00054B/2157